VOLCANIC ERUPTIONS

THE WORST IN HISTORY

BY JENNA VALE

Gareth Stevens
PUBLISHING

Please visit our website, www.garethstevens.com. For a free color catalog of all our high-quality books, call toll free 1-800-542-2595 or fax 1-877-542-2596.

Library of Congress Cataloging-in-Publication Data

Names: Vale, Jenna, author.
Title: Volcanic eruptions : the worst in history / Jenna Vale.
Description: New York : Gareth Stevens Publishing, [2025] | Series: World's worst disasters | Includes bibliographical references and index.
Identifiers: LCCN 2024004863 | ISBN 9781482466768 (library binding) | ISBN 9781482466751 (paperback) | ISBN 9781482466775 (ebook)
Subjects: LCSH: Volcanic eruptions–History–Juvenile literature.
Classification: LCC QE521.3 .V335 2025 | DDC 551.2109–dc23/eng/20240216
LC record available at https://lccn.loc.gov/2024004863

First Edition

Published in 2025 by
Gareth Stevens Publishing
2544 Clinton St
Buffalo, NY 14224

Copyright © 2025 Gareth Stevens Publishing

Portions of this work were originally authored by Janey Levy and published as *World's Worst Volcanic Eruptions*. All new material in this edition is authored by Jenna Vale.

Designer: Claire Zimmermann
Editor: Megan Kellerman

Photo credits: Cover, p. 1 (main photo) DarwelShots/Shutterstock.com; series art (newsprint background) Here/Shutterstock.com; series art (fact box background) levan828/Shutterstock.com; series art (cover & caption box paper texture) Suti Stock Photo/Shutterstock.com; series art (hazard symbol) Maksym Drozd/Shutterstock.com; p. 5 Wead/Shutterstock.com; p. 7 Rainer Lesniewski/Shutterstock.com; p. 8 shooarts/Shutterstock.com; p. 9 Yvonne Baur/Shutterstock.com; p. 11 courtesy of National Park Service; p. 15 Arief Adhari/Shutterstock.com; p. 17 courtesy of U.S. Geological Survey; p. 19 Galih Yoga Wicaksono/Alamy Stock Photo; p. 21 USGS Kīlauea multimediaFile-2444 (2018-07-17).jpg/Wikimedia Commons; p. 23 (upper) courtesy of NASA; p. 23 (lower) Sara Hahn/Shutterstock.com; p. 24 Naeblys/Shutterstock.com; p. 25 ZUMA Press, Inc./Alamy Stock Photo; p. 27 Chanya Thirawarapan/Shutterstock.com; p. 29 Almannavarnadeild/Alamy Stock Photo.

CPSIA compliance information: Batch #CS25GS: For further information contact Gareth Stevens at 1-800-542-2595.

Find us on

CONTENTS

WORDS IN THE GLOSSARY APPEAR IN BOLD THE FIRST TIME THEY ARE USED IN THE TEXT.

EARTH OPENS UP

Volcanoes are one of our planet's most unusual features. They are natural vents in Earth's crust through which steam, hot gases, and hot rocks **erupt**. Volcanoes usually look like mountains, but they don't form the same way mountains do. When a volcano erupts, the materials that come out of it build up, slowly forming the volcano.

Volcanic eruptions can be very dangerous. They send ash and dust into the air. **Lava** flows can spread down a volcano and cause great damage, or harm, to homes, roads, and land. Eruptions can hurt or kill people too. There have been many powerful volcanic eruptions throughout history.

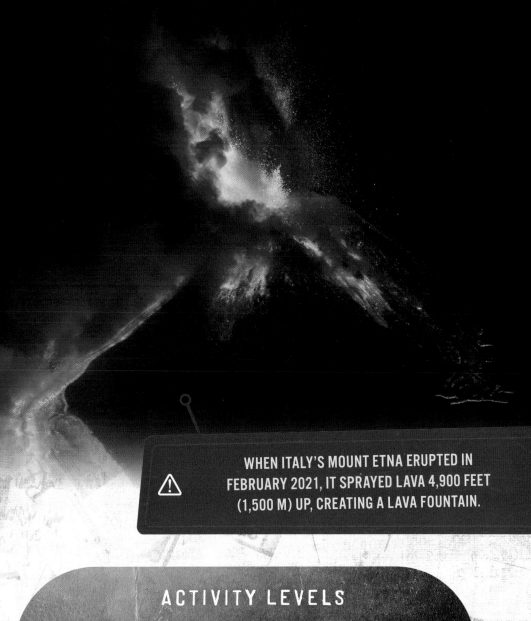

⚠ WHEN ITALY'S MOUNT ETNA ERUPTED IN FEBRUARY 2021, IT SPRAYED LAVA 4,900 FEET (1,500 M) UP, CREATING A LAVA FOUNTAIN.

ACTIVITY LEVELS

VOLCANOES HAVE DIFFERENT ACTIVITY LEVELS. SOME VOLCANOES ARE ACTIVE, WHICH MEANS THEY STILL ERUPT. OTHERS ARE DORMANT, WHICH MEANS THEY HAVE NOT ERUPTED IN A VERY LONG TIME. VOLCANOES THAT HAVEN'T ERUPTED IN THOUSANDS OF YEARS ARE EXTINCT. THESE ACTIVITY LEVELS CAN ALWAYS CHANGE. EVEN DORMANT OR EXTINCT VOLCANOES CAN ERUPT IN THE FUTURE.

ALL OVER THE WORLD

There are volcanoes all around the world. They can be found in Hawaii, Iceland, Africa, and Europe. Some volcanoes are even found on the ocean floor. Most volcanoes, however, are found in a band around the Pacific Ocean called the Ring of Fire.

Volcanoes are sorted into groups based on their shape and what they are made of. Shield volcanoes are low, wide, and made of lava. **Cinder** cones are shaped like cones and made of **tephra**. Another kind of volcano is called a stratovolcano, which is cone-shaped and made of lava and tephra. A stratovolcano is also called a **composite** volcano.

THE RING OF FIRE

EURASIAN
PLATE

JUAN DE FUCA
PLATE

NORTH
AMERICAN
PLATE

CARIBBEAN
PLATE

PHILIPPINE
PLATE

PACIFIC
PLATE

COCOS
PLATE

SOUTH
AMERICAN
PLATE

AUSTRALIAN
PLATE

NAZCA
PLATE

 RING OF FIRE

⚠ THE RED RING SURROUNDING THE PACIFIC
OCEAN IS THE RING OF FIRE. THIS MAP ALSO
SHOWS THE AREA'S TECTONIC PLATES.

TECTONIC PLATES

THE RING OF FIRE IS NEARLY 25,000 MILES
(40,000 KM) LONG. IT FOLLOWS THE EDGES OF SEVERAL
TECTONIC PLATES, WHICH ARE HUGE SLABS OF ROCK IN
EARTH'S TOP TWO LAYERS. THE PLATES MOVE AGAINST
EACH OTHER, CAUSING EARTHQUAKES AND CREATING
THE CONDITIONS FOR VOLCANOES TO FORM.

TAKING
SHAPE

Volcanoes are connected to magma, or hot and melted rock, deep inside the planet. Gas mixed with the magma makes the magma lighter than the rock around it. The magma then rises toward Earth's surface. It melts the rock around it and forms a large space, which is called a magma chamber.

The weight of the rock around the chamber presses on the magma and causes the magma to rise. The magma and gas melt a path to the surface and blast through it. This blast forms a vent. Magma turns to lava when it erupts from the vent. The erupted materials shape the volcano over time.

⚠ WHEN LAVA COOLS, IT HARDENS INTO ROCK. THIS IS HOW VOLCANOES GET THEIR SHAPE AND HEIGHT.

HOT LAVA

LAVA IS INTENSELY HOT, REACHING TEMPERATURES BETWEEN 1,300 AND 2,200°F (700 AND 1,200°C). IT CAN BE VERY THIN, LIKE SYRUP, OR VERY THICK. THE THICKNESS AFFECTS HOW QUICKLY LAVA MOVES. SOME LAVA FLOWS CAN MOVE AS QUICKLY AS 19 MILES (30 KM) PER HOUR. LAVA IS VERY DANGEROUS. IT DESTROYS EVERYTHING IT TOUCHES.

CAUSING DAMAGE

Some eruptions are more powerful than others. Sometimes lava flows quietly, and sometimes it shoots high into the air. Other eruptions blast out tephra and send gases and cinders several miles up. The most powerful eruptions send clouds of hot gases, ash, dust, and tephra rushing down the volcano and may even blow the volcano apart.

Eruptions can cause different kinds of damage and **disaster**. In May 1980, the eruption of Mount St. Helens in Washington State destroyed homes, bridges, and trees over 200 square miles (500 sq km). It killed 57 people and thousands of animals. Mud and **debris** flowed as far as 17 miles (27 km) away from the volcano.

⚠ THE ERUPTION OF MOUNT ST. HELENS IN MAY 1980, SEEN HERE, WAS THE MOST DAMAGING VOLCANIC ERUPTION IN U.S. HISTORY.

MOUNT VESUVIUS

A VOLCANO IN ITALY CALLED MOUNT VESUVIUS IS FAMOUS FOR ITS MANY ERUPTIONS. IN THE YEAR 79, VESUVIUS ERUPTED AND SENT HOT ROCKS, LAVA, AND MUD RACING DOWN ITS SIDE. THE ERUPTION DESTROYED THE CITY OF POMPEII. THE CITY HAD 20,000 PEOPLE LIVING THERE AT THE TIME, AND THOUSANDS OF THEM DIED.

TAMBORA MAKES HISTORY

The largest eruption in recorded history happened in Indonesia, a Southeast Asian country in the Ring of Fire. In April 1815, Indonesia's Mount Tambora erupted. It sent out huge amounts of gas, ash, and a type of tephra called pumice. Homes collapsed under the weight of the ash, and crops died.

The **pyroclastic** flows killed around 11,000 people. At least 100,000 more people died from the hunger and sickness that followed. The dust and ash in the air blocked the sunlight and made the whole planet colder for years. The year after the eruption, 1816, was so cold that people called it the year without a summer.

THE ERUPTION'S IMPACT

1815 — Mount Tambora erupts, causing great destruction and blocking out the sun.

1816 — Rainfall increases and temperatures drop, hurting crops in Europe and causing the year without a summer.

1817 — Colder waters in the Bay of Bengal give rise to a new strain of the disease cholera. Cholera spreads, becoming the world's first pandemic, or global outbreak of an illness.

1818 — Arctic ice that melted after the eruption refreezes. Explorers try and fail to sail through the Arctic for years after. Some of them disappear.

1819 — Farming improves in Europe. Countries buy fewer crops from the United States, causing the first U.S. economic crisis.

 THIS TIMELINE SHOWS SOME OF THE FAR-REACHING IMPACTS OF MOUNT TAMBORA'S ERUPTION.

FLOATING ASH

MOUNT TAMBORA'S ERUPTION LET OUT AROUND 36 CUBIC MILES (150 CU KM) OF ASH, GAS, AND PUMICE. THERE WAS SO MUCH ASH, IT EVEN PILED SEVERAL FEET HIGH ON THE SURFACE OF THE OCEAN. PASSING SHIPS HAD TO PUSH THROUGH THE FLOATING ASH FOR SOME TIME.

KRAKATAU ERUPTS

Nearly 70 years after Mount Tambora erupted, another volcano exploded in the Ring of Fire. Indonesia's Krakatau erupted in August 1883. No people lived on Krakatau's island at the time, but the eruption destroyed most of the island, causing great damage to local plant and animal life.

People as far as 3,000 miles (4,828 km) away from Krakatau heard the powerful eruption. It sent out huge amounts of dust, ash, and pumice. The eruption also caused tsunamis, which are giant ocean waves. Some waves were more than 100 feet (30 m) high. The tsunamis killed around 36,000 people and destroyed coastal towns on nearby islands.

ANOTHER ERUPTION

IN DECEMBER 2018, KRAKATAU ERUPTED AGAIN. THE ERUPTION'S FORCE CAUSED PART OF THE VOLCANO TO BREAK OFF AND FALL INTO THE SEA. THE COLLAPSE CAUSED A TSUNAMI WITH WAVES HIGHER THAN 16 FEET (5 M). THE DISASTER HAPPENED WITHOUT WARNING. IT CAUSED TREMENDOUS DAMAGE TO INDONESIAN COASTAL COMMUNITIES, AND AROUND 430 PEOPLE DIED.

 KRAKATAU HAS ERUPTED MANY TIMES SINCE 1883. THE ERUPTION SEEN HERE HAPPENED IN OCTOBER 2018.

A DEADLY
STORM

One night in November 1985, a volcano called Nevado del Ruiz erupted in the South American country of Colombia. Noise and rain from a storm covered the sound of the explosion and the eruption cloud. The people of the nearby town of Armero had no warning.

An ice cap covers Nevado del Ruiz's top. However, ash, pumice, and lava melted part of the ice cap when the volcano erupted. Water from the melted ice cap caused mudflows, which raced down the volcano. One mudflow was filled with huge rocks that broke a dam and started a flood. The mudflows and flood destroyed Armero and killed around 25,000 people.

⚠ THE MUDFLOWS COMPLETELY COVERED ARMERO, SEEN HERE AFTER THE ERUPTION.

DANGEROUS MUDFLOWS

A VOLCANIC MUDFLOW IS CALLED A LAHAR. WHILE A LAVA FLOW IS HOT, A LAHAR CAN BE HOT OR COLD. WATER AND VOLCANIC ROCKS MIX TOGETHER AND LOOK LIKE WET CONCRETE SLIDING DOWN THE VOLCANO. A LAHAR CAN BECOME BIGGER AS IT PICKS UP MORE DEBRIS ON THE WAY DOWN, MAKING IT VERY DANGEROUS.

MOUNT MERAPI

In October 2010, Mount Merapi erupted for nearly a month in Indonesia. The eruption let out ash, pyroclastic flows, and caused lahars. The strongest explosions happened in early November. Because scientists were studying the volcano, they had plenty of time to alert people so they could **evacuate**. Nearly 350,000 people left the area.

Although so many people were saved, the eruption killed at least 341 people. More than 2,000 homes were destroyed. There were problems even after the eruption stopped. A few months later, lahars flowed back into the valley when there was heavy rain. Around 9,000 people had to evacuate again.

⚠ A SCIENTIST EXPLAINS INDONESIA'S VOLCANIC HISTORY TO CHILDREN WHO LIVE NEAR MOUNT MERAPI SO THEY CAN BE PREPARED FOR THE NEXT ERUPTION.

WARNING SYSTEM

INDONESIA HAS THE HIGHEST RISK FOR VOLCANIC DISASTERS OF ANY COUNTRY IN THE WORLD. BECAUSE OF THIS, SCIENTISTS TAKE STUDYING INDONESIA'S VOLCANIC ACTIVITY VERY SERIOUSLY. LOCAL AND FOREIGN SCIENTISTS WORK TOGETHER TO IMPROVE MEASURING TOOLS, STUDY DATA, AND GET THE WORD OUT IF AN ERUPTION OCCURS.

KĪLAUEA IN 2018

The Hawaiian Islands have a shield volcano called Kīlauea on the big island of Hawaii. In May 2018, Kīlauea erupted. The eruption lasted about four months. It sent a historic amount of lava down the volcano, over the island, and into the ocean. Scientists collected so much data, it would take them years to study everything about the eruption.

Around 2,000 people had to leave the area. Lava flows destroyed more than 700 homes. Even homes left standing could not be lived in because lava had ruined roads, water, and electricity supplies near the volcano. The disaster cost more than $236 million, and it would take years for the island to recover.

⚠️ KĪLAUEA'S ERUPTION PRODUCED SO MUCH LAVA, SCIENTISTS SAID THAT IF THEY COULD COLLECT IT ALL INTO A CUBE, THE CUBE WOULD BE THREE TIMES AS TALL AS NEW YORK CITY'S EMPIRE STATE BUILDING.

KĪLAUEA CRATER

THE TOP OF KĪLAUEA HAS A LARGE CRATER CALLED A CALDERA. SOMETIMES AN ERUPTION CAUSES PARTS OF A VOLCANO TO COLLAPSE. WHEN THE TOP AND SIDES OF A VOLCANO COLLAPSE INWARD, A CALDERA FORMS. WHEN KĪLAUEA ERUPTED IN 2018, PART OF THE CALDERA COLLAPSED, LOWERING ITS FLOOR BY 1,600 FEET (500 M).

VOLCÁN DE FUEGO

The Central American country of Guatemala has a volcano called Volcán de Fuego that erupts frequently. In June 2018, the volcano had one of its biggest eruptions. Satellites could see the eruption's ash **plume** rise as high as 9 miles (15 km) into the sky—high enough to break through the clouds. The ash fell as far as 37 miles (60 km) away from the volcano.

Pyroclastic flows, lahars, and ash covered communities below the volcano. More than 3,200 people evacuated from the area, and more than 200 people died. It was Volcán de Fuego's deadliest eruption in recent history.

⚠️ A NASA SATELLITE CAPTURED THIS IMAGE OF VOLCÁN DE FUEGO'S ASH PLUME FROM ABOVE.

DISASTER RELIEF

BAD WEATHER WAS ONE OF THE REASONS VOLCÁN DE FUEGO'S ERUPTION WAS SO DEADLY. DURING THE ERUPTION, A RAINSTORM HID THE PYROCLASTIC FLOWS FROM SIGHT, SO PEOPLE DID NOT SEE THEM COMING. THE STORM ALSO MADE IT HARDER FOR DISASTER RELIEF TEAMS TO REACH PEOPLE AFTER THE ERUPTION.

VOLCÁN DE FUEGO ERUPTING

UNDERSEA
ERUPTION

In December 2021, an undersea volcano in the Ring of Fire began to erupt. It was the Hunga Tonga–Hunga Ha'apai volcano, which is part of the South Pacific Island country of Tonga. In January 2022, the eruption ended with a massive explosion.

The volcano shot an incredible amount of water vapor into the **atmosphere**, more than any eruption ever before. The water vapor plume rose 36 miles (58 km) into the sky. It was the biggest explosion in the atmosphere ever recorded. Scientists said this volcano could produce such a huge eruption maybe once every 1,000 years.

3D MODEL OF THE ERUPTION

⚠ LOCAL SCIENTISTS, SEEN HERE, MONITORED THE ERUPTION IN JANUARY 2022 FROM A SAFE DISTANCE. THE FINAL EXPLOSION HAPPENED A FEW DAYS LATER.

ACROSS THE OCEAN

THE ERUPTION CAUSED A TSUNAMI THAT FLOODED TONGA AND CAUSED SEVERE DAMAGE. PARTS OF THE COUNTRY LOST POWER, AND TONGA BRIEFLY LOST CONTACT WITH THE REST OF THE WORLD. THE TSUNAMI SURGED ACROSS THE PACIFIC OCEAN, WITH WAVES REACHING AS FAR AWAY AS JAPAN AND CALIFORNIA. THE TSUNAMI KILLED AT LEAST SIX PEOPLE.

VOLCANO SAFETY

Scientists study eruptions, volcanic rocks, and even earthquakes to learn more about a volcano. They use special tools to study activity inside a volcano and tell government leaders if they think an eruption is about to happen. TV, radio, and online news then warns everyone and tells them what to do.

If you live near a volcano, ask your parent or guardian about signing up for alerts to let you know when there is volcanic activity. Make a disaster plan with your family and make sure you have **emergency** supplies at home. These steps will help you stay safe if an eruption happens.

DANGER

VOLCANIC FUMES ARE
HAZARDOUS TO YOUR
HEALTH AND MAY BE
LIFE THREATENING
DO NOT ENTER THIS AREA IF
YOU ARE A PERSON AT RISK

- RESPIRATORY PROBLEMS
- HEART PROBLEMS
- PREGNANT
- INFANTS & YOUNG CHILDREN

⚠ THIS SIGN IN HAWAII WARNS PEOPLE THAT BREATHING IN VOLCANIC FUMES CAN BE DANGEROUS, ESPECIALLY FOR PEOPLE WITH CERTAIN HEALTH CONDITIONS.

SOMETHING IN THE AIR

VOLCANIC DUST AND ASH CAN BE HARMFUL TO
YOUR HEALTH. IF AN ERUPTION PRODUCES A LOT OF DUST
OR ASH, MAKE SURE YOUR WINDOWS AND DOORS ARE CLOSED.
DON'T GO OUTSIDE UNLESS YOU HAVE TO. IF YOU DO HAVE TO
GO OUTSIDE, WEAR A DUST MASK TO LIMIT THE AMOUNT
OF DUST OR ASH YOU INHALE.

VOLCANOES AND CLIMATE

Scientists have found that **climate change** might affect the frequency of volcanic eruptions. They studied the history of eruptions in Iceland and found that when the climate was cooler and there were more glaciers, eruptions happened less often. Less ice and warmer global temperatures may mean more volcanic activity in the future.

Volcanic eruptions will always happen, but climate change can be slowed down. The main cause of climate change is human activity such as burning oil and natural gas for energy. Switching to other energy sources will help slow the changing climate and may stop eruptions from happening more frequently, making everyone safer.

IN JANUARY 2024, LAVA ERUPTED FROM A VENT ON THE EDGE OF A SMALL ICELANDIC VILLAGE.

FURTHER DISASTER

CLIMATE CHANGE IMPACTS MANY NATURAL DISASTERS, INCLUDING WILDFIRES, FLOODS, AND SEVERE STORMS. AS OTHER DISASTERS BECOME WORSE AND MORE FREQUENT, SCIENTISTS THINK IT'S MORE LIKELY THAT VOLCANIC ERUPTIONS WILL HAPPEN AT THE SAME TIME AS OTHER DISASTERS. SLOWING CLIMATE CHANGE WILL HELP DECREASE THE CHANCES OF MULTIPLE DISASTERS HAPPENING AT THE SAME TIME.

GLOSSARY

atmosphere: The mixture of gases that surround a planet.

cinder: A piece of ash or lava from an erupting volcano.

climate change: Long-term change in Earth's climate, caused mainly by human activities such as burning oil and natural gas.

composite: A solid made from two or more kinds of matter.

debris: The remains of something that has been broken.

disaster: An event that causes much suffering or loss.

emergency: An unexpected situation that needs quick action.

erupt: To burst forth.

evacuate: To withdraw from a place for protection.

lava: Melted rock that erupts from a volcano.

plume: Something such as smoke, steam, or water that rises into the air in a tall, thin shape.

pyroclastic: Relating to fragments, or pieces, of ash or lava that have erupted from a volcano.

tephra: Hard matter that has erupted from a volcano.

FOR MORE INFORMATION

BOOKS

Doeden, Matt. *Can You Stop a Volcanic Disaster?* North Mankato, MN: Capstone Press, 2021.

Murray, Julie. *Volcano Geology*. Minneapolis, MN: DASH, 2022.

Williams, Olivia. *Understanding Volcanic Eruptions*. Ann Arbor, MI: Cherry Lake Press, 2022.

WEBSITES

NASA Space Place
spaceplace.nasa.gov/volcanoes2
Learn more about the science of volcanic eruptions with articles, diagrams, and videos.

National Geographic Kids
kids.nationalgeographic.com
Learn more about the science of how volcanoes form and affect our world.

Ready Kids
ready.gov/kids/disaster-facts/volcanoes
Learn more about what to do before, during, and after a volcanic eruption.

Publisher's note to educators and parents: Our editors have carefully reviewed these websites to ensure that they are suitable for students. Many websites change frequently, however, and we cannot guarantee that a site's future contents will continue to meet our high standards of quality and educational value. Be advised that students should be closely supervised whenever they access the internet.

INDEX